BIRD VIEWING AREAS

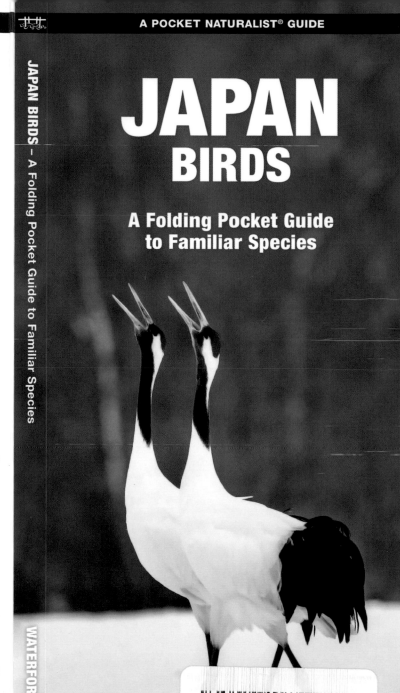

RYUKYU ISLANDS

HOKKAIDO
Sapporo

HONSHU

Osaka

SHIKOKU

■	Coniferous Forest
▨	Deciduous Forest
▨	Broadleaf Evergreen
▨	Alpine Tundra

Japan's diverse habitats – ranging from alpine tundra and dense forests to subtropical islands – support a rich avifauna of more than 610 species, including 13 endemics (found nowhere else) and five breeding endemics (which breed only in Japan). The area is a magnet for migratory birds, which account for 60% of the species found here.

1. Utonai-ko Sanctuary
2. Tateyama Wild Bird Sanctuary
3. Lake Akkeshi & Bekanbeushi Marsh
4. Kushiro-shitsugen National Park
5. Karuizawa Wild Bird Sanctuary
6. Katano Waterfowl Sanctuary
7. Yatsu Higata Nature Observation Center
8. Arasaki Crane Reserve
9. Yoshino-Kumano National Park
10. Kirishima-Yaku National Park
11. Akan National Park
12. Kyoto Imperial Palace Park
13. Rishiri-Rebun-Sarobetsu National Park
14. Hokkaido Ferry
15. Shikotsu-Toya National Park
16. Ukishima Marsh
17. Rikuchu Kaigan National Park
18. Nikko National Park
19. Atsumi Peninsula
20. Fuji-Hakone-Izu National Park
21. Miyakejima
22. Okinawa
23. National Museum of Nature and Science
24. Shimokita Peninsula

$7.95 U.S.
$9.95 CAN
ISBN 978-1-62005-276-1
50795
9 781620 052761
UPC 8 84682 01263 2
10 9 8 7 6 5 4 3 2 1
Made in the USA
T0123999

A POCKET NATURALIST® GUIDE

JAPAN BIRDS

A Folding Pocket Guide to Familiar Species

JAPAN BIRDS – A Folding Pocket Guide to Familiar Species

WATERFORD PRESS

WATERBIRDS & NEARSHORE BIRDS

Pacific Diver
Gavia pacifica
To 25 in. (63 cm)
Winter / Summer

Little Grebe
Tachybaptus ruficollis
To 12 in. (30 cm)
Note thin bill.

Black-throated Diver
Gavia arctica To 27 in. (68 cm)
Note white flank patch.
Winter / Summer

Great Crested Grebe
Podiceps cristatus
To 20 in. (50 cm)
Winter / Summer

Mallard
Anas platyrhynchos
To 28 in. (70 cm)
♀ ♂

Whooper Swan
Cygnus cygnus
To 5 ft. (1.5 m)
Yellow bill patch extends to the nostrils.

Mute Swan
Cygnus olor To 5 ft. (1.5 m)
Introduced resident species.

Eurasian Wigeon
Anas penelope
To 20 in. (50 cm)
♀ ♂

Baikal Teal
Anas formosa To 17 in. (43 cm)
♀ ♂

Common Teal
Anas crecca To 15 in. (38 cm)

Spot-billed Duck
Anas zonorhyncha To 25 in. (63 cm)
Bill has a yellow tip.

WATERBIRDS & NEARSHORE BIRDS

Goosander
Mergus merganser To 27 in. (68 cm)
Note thin bill.

Tufted Duck
Aythya fuligula To 17 in. (43 cm)
Note prominent head crest. Common winter visitor.
♀

Mandarin Duck
Aix galericulata
To 20 in. (50 cm)

Black-crowned Night-Heron
Nycticorax nycticorax
To 28 in. (70 cm)

Sanderling
Calidris alba
To 8 in. (20 cm)
Runs in and out with waves along shorelines.
Non-breeding plumage

Northern Lapwing
Vanellus vanellus
To 12 in. (30 cm)

Ruddy Turnstone
Arenaria interpres
To 10 in. (25 cm)

Eurasian Oystercatcher
Haematopus ostralegus
To 18 in. (45 cm)

Black-winged Stilt
Himantopus himantopus
To 15 in. (38 cm)

Kentish Plover
Charadrius alexandrinus
To 6 in. (15 cm)

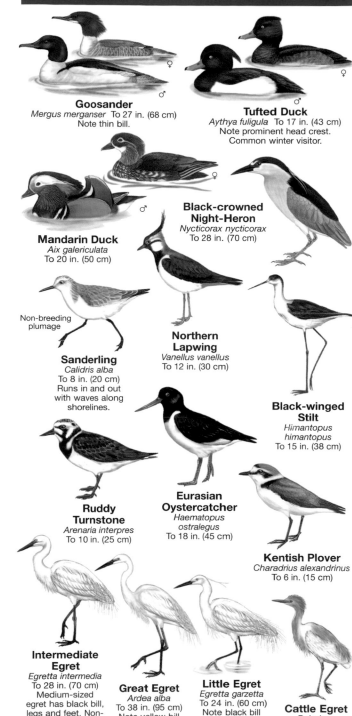

Intermediate Egret
Egretta intermedia
To 28 in. (70 cm)
Medium-sized egret has black bill, legs and feet. Non-breeding birds have a yellow bill with a black tip.

Great Egret
Ardea alba
To 38 in. (95 cm)
Note yellow bill and black feet.

Little Egret
Egretta garzetta
To 24 in. (60 cm)
Note black bill and yellow feet.

Cattle Egret
Bubulcus coromandus
To 20 in. (50 cm)

WATERBIRDS & NEARSHORE BIRDS

Gray Heron
Ardea cinerea
To 38 in. (95 cm)

White-naped Crane
Grus vipio
To 52 in. (1.3 m)

Common Crane
Grus grus
To 4 ft. (1.2 m)

Red-crowned Crane
Grus japonensis
To 5 ft. (1.5 m)
Also called Japanese crane.

Crested Kingfisher
Megaceryle lugubris
To 15 in. (38 cm)

Common Kingfisher
Alcedo atthis
To 7 in. (18 cm)

Laysan Albatross
Phoebastria immutabilis
To 32 in. (80 cm)

Ancient Murrelet
Synthliboramphus antiquus
To 11 in. (28 cm)
Note white plume over eye.
Winter

Brown Booby
Sula leucogaster
To 30 in. (75 cm)

Great Cormorant
Phalacrocorax carbo
To 40 in. (1 m)
Back is glossy black.

Common Gallinule
Gallinula chloropus
To 14 in. (35 cm)

Spectacled Guillemot
Cepphus carbo
To 15 in. (38 cm)

Japanese Cormorant
Phalacrocorax capillatus
To 34 in. (85 cm)
Back is green-black. Note shortish tail. Endemic.

Eurasian Coot
Fulica atra To 16 in. (40 cm)

Rhinoceros Auklet
Cerorhinca monocerata
To 15 in. (38 cm)
Resident has upturned facial plumes.

WATERBIRDS & NEARSHORE BIRDS

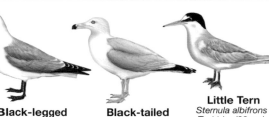

Black-legged Kittiwake
Rissa tridactyla
To 18 in. (45 cm)
Legs and wing tips are black.

Black-tailed Gull
Larus crassirostris
To 19 in. (48 cm)

Little Tern
Sternula albifrons
To 11 in. (28 cm)

DOVES, PHEASANTS, ETC.

Oriental Turtle Dove
Streptopelia orientalis
To 13 in. (33 cm)
Note neck stripes.

White-bellied Green Pigeon
Treron sieboldii
To 13 in. (33 cm)

Little Cuckoo
Cuculus poliocephalus
To 10 in. (25 cm)
Note small size.

Oriental Cuckoo
Cuculus saturatus
To 13 in. (33 cm)

Japanese Quail
Coturnix japonica
To 7.5 in. (19 cm)

Chinese Bamboo Partridge
Bambusicola thoracica
To 11 in. (28 cm)

White-rumped Swift
Apus pacificus
To 8 in. (20 cm)

Copper Pheasant
Syrmaticus soemmerringii
To 50 in. (1.25 m)
Endemic.

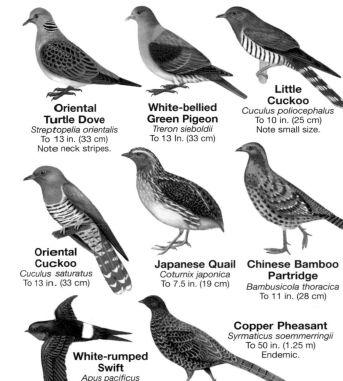

Japanese Green Pheasant
Phasianus versicolor
To 32 in. (80 cm)
Endemic species is national bird of Japan.

Common Pheasant
Phasianus colchicus
To 3 ft. (90 cm)
Introduced resident species is a common resident on Hokkaido and Tsushima.

BIRDS OF PREY

Steller's Sea Eagle
Haliaeetus pelagicus
To 40 in. (1 m)
Locally common in northern Japan.

Eurasian Sparrowhawk
Accipiter nisus
To 16 in. (40 cm)
Note long, barred tail.

Osprey
Pandion haliaetus
To 2 ft. (60 cm)
Fish-eating raptor is a common resident.

Golden Eagle
Aquila chrysaetos
To 40 in. (1 m)
Nests in mountains on rocky ledges.

Goshawk
Accipiter gentilis
To 2 ft. (60 cm)
Note dark cap and white "eyebrow."

Japanese Sparrowhawk
Accipiter gularis
To 11 in. (28 cm)
Japan's smallest hawk.

Oriental Honey Buzzard
Pernis ptilorhynchus
To 26 in. (65 cm)
Note small head and short crest.

Peregrine Falcon
Falco peregrinus
To 20 in. (50 cm)

Merlin
Falco columbarius
To 14 in. (35 cm)
Note small size. Tail is heavily banded.

Gray-faced Buzzard
Butastur indicus
To 20 in. (50 cm)
White throat has central black stripe.

Black Kite
Milvus migrans
To 22 in. (55 cm)
Note flash of white on underwings. The most common hawk in Japan.

Common Kestrel
Falco tinnunculus
To 14 in. (35 cm)
Small falcon.

BIRDS OF PREY

Common Buzzard
Buteo buteo
To 25 in. (63 cm)
Plumage may be dark or light brown.

Ural Owl
Strix uralensis
To 2 ft. (60 cm)

Brown Hawk Owl
Ninox scutulata
To 12 in. (30 cm)

WOODPECKERS

Great Spotted Woodpecker
Dendrocopos major
To 10 in. (25 cm)
Note reddish undertail feathers.

Japanese Green Woodpecker
Picus awokera
To 12 in. (30 cm)
Endemic.

Japanese Pygmy Woodpecker
Picoides kizuki
To 6 in. (15 cm)

PERCHING BIRDS

Winter Wren
Troglodytes troglodytes
To 4 in. (10 cm)

Asian House Martin
Delichon dasypus
To 5 in. (13 cm)

Goldcrest
Regulus regulus
To 4 in. (10 cm)
Tiny woodland bird has an orange-yellow crown stripe.

Sand Martin
Riparia riparia
To 6 in. (15 cm)
Note breast band.

Ashy Minivet
Pericrocotus divaricatus
To 8 in. (20 cm)

Barn Swallow
Hirundo rustica
To 8 in. (20 cm)
Note deeply forked tail.

PERCHING BIRDS

Bull-headed Shrike
Lanius bucephalus
To 8 in. (20 cm)

Brown Shrike
Lanius cristatus
To 8 in. (20 cm)

Asian Stubtail
Urosphena squameiceps
To 4 in. (10 cm)

Varied Tit
Sittiparus varius
To 6 in. (15 cm)

Great Tit
Parus major
To 6 in. (15 cm)
Note black stripe down center of breast.

Long-tailed Tit
Aegithalos caudatus
To 6 in. (15 cm)

Coal Tit
Periparus ater
To 5 in. (13 cm)
Note white nape.

Willow Tit
Poecile montanus
To 5 in. (13 cm)

Brown-eared Bulbul
Hypsipetes amaurotis
To 11 in. (28 cm)

Waxwing
Bombycilla spp.
To 8 in. (20 cm)
Red wing marks look like waxy droplets.

Red-flanked Bluetail
Tarsiger cyanurus
To 6 in. (15 cm)

Japanese Wagtail
Motacilla grandis
To 8 in. (20 cm)
Endemic.

White Wagtail
Motacilla alba
To 8 in. (20 cm)
Constantly wags its tail when foraging on the ground.

Gray Wagtail
Motacilla cinerea
To 8 in. (20 cm)

PERCHING BIRDS

Eurasian Nuthatch
Sitta europaea
To 6 in. (15 cm)
Often seen crawling along tree trunks in search of insects.

Treecreeper
Certhia familiaris
To 5 in. (13 cm)
Usually seen foraging for insects on tree trunks.

Pale Thrush
Turdus pallidus
To 10 in. (25 cm)

Brown-headed Thrush
Turdus chrysolaus
To 9 in. (23 cm)

White's Thrush
Zoothera dauma
To 12 in. (30 cm)
Note large size.

Japanese Thrush
Turdus cardis
To 9 in. (23 cm)

Japanese Robin
Erithacus akahige
To 6 in. (15 cm)

Blue Rock Thrush
Monticola solitarius
To 10 in. (25 cm)

Brown Dipper
Cinclus pallasii
To 9 in. (23 cm)

Azure-winged Magpie
Cyanopica cyanus
To 14 in. (35 cm)

Daurian Redstart
Phoenicurus auroreus
To 6 in. (15 cm)

Japanese Accentor
Prunella rubida
To 6 in. (15 cm)

Zitting Cisticola
Cisticola juncidis
To 5 in. (13 cm)
Song is a rapid, repeating – *zip–zip*.

Olive-backed Pipit
Anthus hodgsoni
To 6 in. (15 cm)

PERCHING BIRDS

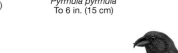

Narcissus Flycatcher
Ficedula narcissina
To 5 in. (13 cm)

Blue-and-white Flycatcher
Cyanoptila cyanomelana
To 6.5 in. (17 cm)

Japanese Paradise Flycatcher
Terpsiphone atrocaudata
To 18 in. (45 cm)

Rook
Corvus frugilegus
To 18 in. (45 cm)
Note gray patch at base of beak.

Carrion Crow
Corvus corone
To 20 in. (50 cm)

Large-billed Crow
Corvus macrorhynchos
To 2 ft. (60 cm)

Japanese White-eye
Zosterops japonicus
To 5 in. (13 cm)
Endemic.

Siberian Stonechat
Saxicola maurus
To 5 in. (13 cm)

Brambling
Fringilla montifringilla
To 6 in. (15 cm)

Japanese Grosbeak
Eophona personata
To 9 in. (23 cm)

Eurasian Jay
Garrulus glandarius
To 14 in. (35 cm)
Note blue wing patch and white rump.

Eurasian Skylark
Alauda arvensis
To 7 in. (18 cm)
Known for the long-lasting, melodious song the male gives on the wing.

White-cheeked Starling
Sturnus cineraceus
To 10 in. (25 cm)
Known for its monotonous call of creaking notes.

PERCHING BIRDS

Eurasian Tree Sparrow
Passer montanus
To 6 in. (15 cm)

Russet Sparrow
Passer rutilans
To 6 in. (15 cm)

Oriental Reed Warbler
Acrocephalus orientalis
To 8 in. (20 cm)

Arctic Warbler
Phylloscopus borealis
To 5 in. (13 cm)
Note prominent "eyebrow."

Eastern Crowned Willow Warbler
Phylloscopus coronatus
To 5 in. (13 cm)

Black-browed Reed Warbler
Acrocephalus bistrigiceps
To 5 in. (13 cm)

Meadow Bunting
Emberiza cioides
To 6.5 in. (17 cm)
Japan's most common bunting.

Japanese Gray Bunting
Emberiza variabilis
To 6 in. (15 cm)

Japanese Bush Warbler
Cettia diphone
To 6 in. (15 cm)

Long-tailed Rosefinch
Uragus sibiricus
To 6 in. (15 cm)

Eurasian Bullfinch
Pyrrhula pyrrhula
To 6 in. (15 cm)

Eurasian Siskin
Spinus spinus
To 6 in. (15 cm)

Oriental Greenfinch
Carduelis sinica
To 6 in. (15 cm)

Red Crossbill
Loxia curvirostra
To 7 in. (18 cm)
Bill is crossed near the tip.